I0662132

These Extremes

Southern Messenger Poets

DAVE SMITH, SERIES EDITOR

Poems and Prose

These Extremes

RICHARD BAUSCH

Louisiana State University Press)((Baton Rouge

Published by Louisiana State University Press
Copyright © 2009 by Richard Bausch
All rights reserved
Manufactured in the United States of America

LSU Press Paperback Original

Designer: Michelle A. Neustrom
Typeface: MrsEaves

LIBRARY OF CONGRESS CATALOGING-IN-PUBLICATION DATA
Bausch, Richard, 1945–
    These extremes : poems and prose / Richard Bausch.
      p. cm. — (Southern messenger poets)
    ISBN 978-0-8071-3521-1 (pbk. : alk. paper)
    I. Title.
    PS3552.A846T49 2010
    811'.54—dc22
                                        2009013854

"Barbara (1943–1974)" first appeared in the *Southern Review* as "Her Photographs."
"Two Handwritten Pages" first appeared in *Five Points.*

The paper in this book meets the guidelines for permanence and durability of
the Committee on Production Guidelines for Book Longevity of the Council
on Library Resources. ♾

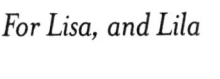

For Lisa, and Lila

Contents

I WAR

Again

At Monte Cassino,
    south of Rome,
Not long before
    the end of the second
War, lines of hardened
    combat veterans
Melted into hospital
    wards, weeping.

The year before
    I was born,
The Germans shot
    thousands of Polish
Civilians even as
    the Russian army
Stood by and watched.

In trenches along the Rhine,
    soldiers sickened
And trembled, and terror roamed
    the churned earth
With the smoke.

These men left home believing in love.
They returned home without the ability
    to believe in love.

That winter of the burning
    snows, the year I was born,
Cities were incinerated.
    Salt of the sea-tide,
Salt of the blood-sea
    loosed upon the world.

Disintegration in an eye-blink,
    the beat of one heart,
One beat. Universes of tender dreams
    up in smoke.
Loves wrapped in ash.

And it is all here again
    for the blood of the abstractions,
Objects of mind, icebergs of thinking.
    The nullifying ideas,
Philosophies.
    Creeds. Beliefs.

I abjure them all, every one.
    We abjure them, all,
Do we not, yet they stay.

Nothing is easier to say
    than that we deplore it. We grieve
To see the whole thing played
    out again and our grief is like
Ritual observance, a rite,
    While all over the world

The tribes and their killers slaughter
    loveliness.

Dark of the sea at night,
    veiled by moonless distance
And the swell of the pulling tides
and the flashing at the horizon
Is beautiful. But it is shell
    bursts, blooms of fire.

In the name of God! *In the name of God.*
    Yes. Oh, yes. That.
In His name, or in the name of Allah
    or party or Country
Or money or madness and it is
    too common for any more speech.

    Murder on that scale,
And this cry itself, this lament
achieves no single element
Of anything new to say. We say this,
we say and say this—and
It is nothing, nothing new.

These men left home believing in love.
In the name of God!

II LEI FLOWER

Poem

Light on blue
Hills, these mountains
As yearnings come,
Colors in treetops
When breezes shift.

Tilt your head
With its dark hair
& little worlds
Under the bones
That will be ashes
Collide.

Sigh sorrowfully,
Once, & the violent
Inward winds
Rise.

Open your hands,
& a starling makes
Its strange, thoughtful,
Lone way to water, while
Songs unwind from
The heavy branches—
Those mild breezes
Of the heaped season.

All this happens.
You do not admit it.
You have scruples.
You are practical
& theories bore you.

This is all perfectly
You. I have complete
Understanding of it.

High Overhead

High overhead,
White on black:

Galaxies.

Milk strewn in swirls
Of suns, spun light,
An infinite
Shore,

Light years gone, distant
As thought
Of the world's end.

Unimaginable darks
Beyond these
Liquefactions of starlight.

Dark as the unfathomable
Darks of your eyes,
               my tender one.

Where you sleep now, this night,
I imagine the bed.
The little stillnesses in your breath,
Each sigh like a wish.

I love you across the cold spaces
Of this world,
               bereft of your voice.

Tonight I'm imagining
That you are imagining me.

There Are Prayers

There are prayers
For which
Prayer
Is no good.

There are hopes
Made out
Of hopelessness,
& the expression
Of them
Is a desolation.

There are ways
The heart longs
For desire while
Closing down love,
& the torments
Stretch long
& far forever.

There are obsessions
Whose brand on the soul
Expresses nothing
But the life not lived.

There are dyings
That are not Death,
& the hell
Of knowing this
Is Hell.

There are loves
Only sayable
Over months

& years
Of holding on.

Ask me tomorrow,
Little one.

Our Mississippi

The river in late afternoon sun shimmers,
Though the water itself, up close, is muddy,
Coffee-colored on the calmest days.

The banks are weedy, & flat barges glide
Along on it like gigantic crocs.

It's easy to believe the whole length of it
Is the same tawny color, with the same wide
Lines of darker currents in its sides.

Here's the flat
Muddy Island we watch from in Memphis—

Bridges & cranes lift toward the edge of the city.

But we know the river mouths its way
A thousand miles from snowy cliffs
& through rocks & down winding branches
Of itself, clear & ice cold, rushing white.

Storms move like love across the surface of it.
                    If the little waves now look
Unhealthy, darkened, smelling of the bitter sea,
There are curves of this same water in bright sun,

Miles north of us, clear as infant sleep.

Snow settles on calm curves of it at one end,
Quiet as thought, & the water speeds to rapids
Hammering rocks in its middle coursing,

Just as, in the calming turns of the south,
Gulls sail & dive over its clear & peaceful shallows. . . .
It's the same water altogether.

I love you as this river is long & beautiful.

When our waters are cloudy there are
Shimmerings still in the other tributaries
Of us, at the source, where we are always,
Dearest, through all weathers, flowing.

Frangipani

Plumeria, it is called
        by the scientists,
    the Lei flower, flower of welcome, flower
                of elegant greeting, of the equator,
        the South American
                forests, the warm green mists.
    Some grow to amazing heights,
            thirty or forty feet.
Frangipani. My love's favorite flower.
    Oh, it would be extravagantly shaped, high-spirited,
                rowdily formed, a pretty flower on a tree
        growing into the hot
                southern sky of an equatorial
island in the sea.
    Frangipani. I hear your happy
                voice saying the word. I like the sound of it
        entirely. Your flower,
                & there is no flower on this fractious
        earth nearly as lovely,
    lei of my soul. There you are, my lissome spirit, all
            inspiring scents: jasmine, citrus, spices, gardenia
            & earth & blossom, oh,
                how the Polynesian
    islanders treasure the large-leafed Frangipani,
                long-petaled, brightly fragrant bloom, on fire
                with summer mornings, giving off the heart
        of paradise in its aromas, our flower,
                excellent as tender colors
        of twilight on the sea,
    tall & pretty, aromatic,
        sweet as breaking dawn
            at the edge
        of that same sea.

III HER PICTURES

Barbara (1943–1974)

1

She's seven years old here, missing the two
Adult teeth. There was a man selling rides
On a Shetland, walking our neighborhood.

The pony's round as a barrel. I don't remember
How she rode him or what we paid to refuse,
Our father coaxing. The one of us not afraid

To go, she sits there squinting into the light,
Laughing or crying. That's me in tennis shoes.
I'm terrified, packing down the wish to be

A cowboy of dreams on a miniature horse,
Dun-eyed pony, prancer and snorter.
If she's laughing it's nervous, almost frantic.

I know from all the years that she liked
To go out and see what might happen
In this world where what happens, happens,

And then happens again and again
In memory, where nothing is accidental.
It's possible that she's crying in this image;

You can't tell from the angle of sun—the slant
Of shadow across her, the elemental
Dimness of sepia—just how she feels.

2

How white the shrine at her shoulder is
Where she holds a bouquet of white roses in both
Hands, like an offering. The light blue ribbons

Trail from her wrists. There are other roses
Blooming toward her, but she doesn't see them.
A day in early spring, bright as Easter,

First Communion. A passage that can't reach her
Yet: summers are endless, hours graduate into
Dinner and sleep: a birthday is important as it

Must be, and Christmas divides each long year.
The statue behind her is of the Virgin
Astride the snake-wrapped globe of the world.

This is a ceremony we may not choose to recall,
But it makes the true division for her, because
She's understood to be at the age of reason.

Capable of the fall from Grace. In all she'll
Find to do she'll work to strengthen her belief.
By the time it touches *us,* this sacrament

Will have failed to hold us together for so long
We'll almost have forgotten the reason for roses.
These blossoms, open, just beneath her throat.

3

She only wants to think she's not alone.
She wears white gloves, lightly touches the mantel
—her hand is already lovely, a woman's hand

Curved, that sharp angle of slender fingers
On the scalloped, polished wooden ledge.
This is someone else's house. She's so close

To being grown, here, with another girl
Whose parents are less strict—it's in the dress,
The differences of dress. The friend makes out,

Stays late where other friends are free to go.
And who can tell this girl in her white gloves,
The first daughter, that her parents are learning

To be parents on her? Not long after this
My sister learns marriage. And later, when her
Water breaks in the first hour of waking, years

From home, still young, surprised, she knows
She can refuse no part of it. Life bears down
On her, and pain she has only ever imagined

Leans in, insisting on itself. She's nineteen,
A girl giving birth to another girl, under the white
Light of Delivery, 1963—doctor, nurses surround her.

And her young husband in another room, on another
Floor, smoking, talking to her father and brothers,
An unreal something happening far away.

Now, as pain reaches another level, the world is
Unbelievably near. The dark opens a new crevice
With each searing breath. And she accepts it all.

4

Yearbook photographs give the lie to faces
And this one lies too well. The touch-up shows,
The professional's botched attempt to coax

An ill-understood feature out of blurred light,
Or the inadequate shade. The smile is strangely
Not hers, though you hear her voice, looking

At it. The dark red hair arranged as it would be
In mid-century, just before the missiles and the
Assassinations. She graduated and drove

In a wild car with friends to the beach,
And came back sunburned, with a boy she planned
To marry—for that was how it was done, then.

The ancient pattern of repeated things
That now we can't believe will stay long, as we
Can't make anything stay, not even the few

Sad things we learn. She married, and we watched
Her go. We mourned her and forgot. But this
Image is not her face. If we'd used those years

She lived not ten miles away, children come
And a house and sorrow, the boy she loved grown
To regret, and an obsession with work,

The grass fresh cut and a neighbor's locked
Unentered doors at night; the little stoop where
She sat out under the hot starry sky in summer,

And smoked, listening to the whoosh of traffic
Off beyond the backyard tree, waiting for him—
If we had used those years we might have more

Than this: trying to look through the artifice
Of a photograph, to gauge that face, the woman
In the blue eyes, looking back at us from there.

I think of her sitting in the cooling dark,
Her children asleep, a record scratching
At the end of a strand, the one small cough

From the bedroom window over the bush:
Her waiting there in the bug-circled light
Searching for a glimmer far down the street,

Blowing the cigarette smoke and hearing
Her own breath. Later, it was in her talk:
You hear so many little noises sitting out alone

On a summer night. I used to watch the lights
Go by past the houses at the end of our road.
I kept thinking one of them might turn in . . .

Oh, I know there were all the sweet times
That anyone has, with children. But
Even those must've seemed diluted by

The sorrow of going through them alone.
The sweetest pass must've been attended with
An ache for loving witnesses. She shouldn't

Have had to wonder why we never visited.
Oh, if I had come to her then! The second of her
Younger brothers—if I had been that moving

Glimmer, turning in, I could close my eyes
Now and begin to tell you, I could close
My eyes and see her human, lovely face.

I see this: I'm looking through fogged glass,
The passenger-window of his car, under
The skeletal shadow of the street lamp

In front of our house. Our mother has sent
Me out to call them in, worried that she's
Staying too long out there alone with this boy.

Worried about appearances, the lure of sex.
I stand outside the car, knowing this, feeling it,
And frightened of it, too—filled with wonder

That she's in love, she's where I long
To go: I peer through a gauzy shimmer
And see her covered hip, the outside curve

Of one exposed thigh—her eyes are closed, her
Mouth open on his. They're not aware of me,
Or anyone. They move against each other

And shift under the shadow of my lifted
Hand, as I begin to think of knocking
And decide I can't. I falter, take the quick

Steps back, slipping into the dark behind
Them, making my way back to the house.
I'll never speak of it. I've learned private life.

Later, sleepless, I can't unthink love
As an impoverished struggle in the stale air
Of closed cars, on gloomy streets of towns

Like ours—this without words. That's how despair
Happens. I always wanted more for us,
Wanted to have loved her enough to guess

She might yearn to see me on those nights
When she waited alone for anyone to come,
The neighborhood dogs barking, moths banging

On glass, the moving glow of cars out on
The interstate, the yellow light above
An aluminum door, leading narrowly into

A house across the street, where a man leaned
To kiss his children good-night. Those lives! Did she
Recall, then, the glare of a skinny street lamp,

The cramped front seat of a '56 Ford?
Did she feel that something had betrayed her, while
She watched for us, and smoked?

5

This is her wedding. Our father and uncles
And their father, posing for the first time
All together, in front of the towering cake.

She may have taken this one. She said later
There would never be another quite like that—
These men with uniformly protruding ears,

"Like a row of taxis with their doors
Wide open." One got drunk, one ate too much
And threw up in the stairwell, and one cried

Sentimental tears, and our father shook
The hand of the groom, whom he had already
Helped find a job, selling cars in the city.

Two of the uncles argued about golf.
There was a record player for the Wedding
March, the swing music everyone knew—

Father loved torch songs, and appreciated
The variety of feeling in that music.
Music with wit, he said, humming Cole Porter.

He teased us about rock, while saxophones,
Clarinets and trumpets melted
Into the musty air of the church basement.

She danced with our grandfather, about whom
I said, "He just goes on and on," and meant
That somehow we all would, too: she waltzed

With him; they murmured pleasantly; he gave
Advice, and then our youngest brother touched
The old man's elbow, cutting in. Only seven,

He didn't reach her waist, quite. They turned
In a small circle of slowly wavering steps,
Like statues coming loose from their moorings,

The boy gazing up at his older sister's face,
Seeming almost frightened, while everyone
Stood watching—how seriously he danced,

Worried, concentrating, thinking through each
Movement. She began crying, her tears so sudden
I thought (as I told her) she'd changed her mind.

6

I wonder if she thought she should have changed
Her mind. Years after, when I was the groom,
In a Midwestern town far from home, she sent

A card; she couldn't travel with three small
Babies, another on the way: *"Assume
Nothing; remember to give and give and give,*

*And keep on giving all the time. That's how
It works."* And I remembered riding out
In the Maryland night, with her husband

Once, six years after her wedding. He talked.
His talk was the point of a buried shout:
"Don't ever get married, man. Don't ever

Have kids." I wondered what he must be like
In the house, what they were like together,
And I was frightened for them both. At my

Wedding, our mother counseled religion,
My future in-laws talked about the weather;
My younger brothers made me laugh—both old

Enough to smoke, though the youngest still
Lacked permission. Did I mention that I
Had been godfather by proxy to her

Second child? Spiritual parent to
A boy I'd never seen, or been seen by.
Before I'd meet him he'd be the same age

As the small boy dancing at the wedding.
How she wept, bending to embrace that child,
Her brother, whom she had mothered, too. They

Held tight, and I took the picture. I keep
Returning to it. She cries through her smile,
Celebrating. But, here, this one, of the men,

Standing happily abreast, arm in arm,
Father, uncles, the family's head—
You see the happy family we once were.

Even the women say so. And this first
Of the family's children to wed
Brought all sides of the family together.

She would do so one other time—twelve years
From that day, though Grandfather was dead
Six years by then, and even we had come

To know we were scattering. Oh, we knew.
On the flight home, coming to say good-bye,
In the black cold cars where we didn't speak,

Riding long behind her, as they carried
Her farther away from home than each lie
Could say *was* home: Death is not a place.

7

This is one she took. Her Christmas. All four
Children happily favor her. The third
Is twin to the girl on the toy horse,

The gray-eyed Shetland pony. Fine
Dark strands of hair upswept in an absurd
Small knot just at the level of her ear.

How odd that, gazing at this face, I can't
Quite recall the face of the living girl
As she was to me once. As she looked when,

Certain of myself, certain of the proofs
Of all surfaces, I told her the world
Was inside a ball, the sky a blue sphere,

And the sun was a light through a small hole
That went away each night, or dimmed till it
Was the moon. *"Silly,"* she said, *"the world is*

The ball. And we're all on the surface." She
Was haughty, since the adults deemed her fit
For such knowledge as I was not. (Am not.)

But this picture was taken, no doubt,
To show all of us. We were ten miles away
And she snapped this picture and we never

Saw it while she lived. We live where the clans
Die out, and no one remembers to say
The names of parents' parents to children.

8

Have I said she wanted to write? She did.
She wrote about fear for her children,
The world's thousand sicknesses, the accidents

Of a moment's inattention. She wrote
About her best friend, who made her laugh.
She planned a mystery and set down verse.

She wrote me letters: *Just imagine, my brother*
Writing poetry! Will you send me more? She suffered
Losses: *Sweetie, I must tell you that I lost the baby*

This week. The doctor says if I'd gone full
term there's no telling what might have happened—
Something went wrong in the beginning . . .

Something went wrong in the beginning.
The beginning was the word and something
Went wrong in the beginning. The word was

With God and the word *was* God, and light
Shineth in the darkness. Oh, I have so
Little from when we were both in the world.

9

There aren't very many photographs
Finally, nothing like a lifetime's worth.
Barbara Ann. February 9, 1943

—September 28, 1974.
I was in Iowa City, fearing for sanity,
Mine, the minutes turning on dread,

And I had prayed for something other than
That to worry about. All around me
Were the hills of what felt like a foreign

Country, and I had conceived a terror
Of my own mind, its starts and leaps, its awful
Turns, its perverse latitudes, its lightning

Images of death, the harm I might do—
Fear of madness becomes a madness, and
An anxiety I hadn't understood

Worked its way into all my days and nights.
I couldn't think of anything but myself.
My wife and child were hostages to this,

I felt cut off from them, and was appalled
By what I couldn't feel. I was strangeness,
Walking out into the farm-smelling night,

A lone man moving past the windows of
Houses where people lived like another
Species. I understood nothing of how

They managed to get through the days without
Committing suicide. I thought of that,
Thought of suicide. I even planned it,

How I'd cancel everything, making it
Look like an accident. I'd step in front
Of a moving car, or find some poison

That would hide in my blood. Anything but
Madness, which would be violent, and cause
Harm to the people of my little house.

In the middle of this, your letters seemed
To come from some hopeless distance, a kind
Of innocence, an almost obdurate

Busyness, and the assumption that I
Was who I'd been before I left home.
Home: the word had no meaning for me,

Because I couldn't be home anywhere.
I was studying sickness, longing for
Something to wrench me back to some version

Of myself, some semblance of the life I
Thought I was living. I hoped for outside
Force. It came in the form of news that you

Were gone, a ringing telephone in the hour
Before sunrise, and I woke fearing
Heart attack, my wife's father or our own.

I knew it was bad, and knew also that it
Was somehow, awfully, what I'd prayed for,
Coming, as answered prayers do, from some

Unexpected quarter. It wasn't the fathers:
You were no more. I thought of the four children,
Knelt at my bedside in the dawn, reached across

The rumpled sheets, clasped my hands and tried,
Crying, to pray. I said the lines we had
Both learned growing up in a devout house

—the Hail Mary, the Lord's Prayer. The words
Went out of me in sobs, and were just sound,
The deep cough and animal sputter of grief.

10

I saw your breasts once. You were sixteen. I'd
Come past the open window off the back
Steps, in summer, and you were there, just out

Of the bath, toweling off, your hair wrapped
In another towel. I saw your pale
Shoulders, and you turned. How surprised

I was—astonished. The dry grass at my
Feet seemed to stretch noisily to my thighs;
The shade dropped down from the maple tree

Like fallen cloth. But I can't remember you,
That girl, a new woman in my new eyes,
Who was my sister. I can't recover

That girl, that woman. We age, here, and our
Dead mount up. The first of one's deaths recedes
Into the background with wounds and Time.

You're with a populace that increases, too.
I hope you have some sight of those whose
Silence compliments your own. The pictures

In their way are loud. It strikes me that I
Am still hemmed-in by my own sight, my life
Whose borders are narrowing. My selfish

Love, my memory of that other world.
Here, you stand half in, half out of the sea,
Glimmering with lotion. You're waiting for

Something beautiful to happen. You know
It will happen—it has happened to you
Before. And you're ready. You feel certain

We'll be there when the bad years come. You
Aren't afraid. The car's safe. Your husband's
Good with them. Machines work as bodies

Work. The world's sky-blue. You've baptized your
Children. No one's gone. With us, you keep
The holy hour. Sun fires each strand of your hair!

IV BACK STORIES

The Woman in Sargent's
The Sulphur Match Speaks

Well, Dear, we're not petit bourgeois.
We spend the long night hours
In cafés off dim back streets—is
This good? You like my shoes?

Don't question the first aspect of this
Crazed time. The congregations
Sleep. There's no rest for the likes of us
While moonlight bathes the town.

Oh, if I wish to wear a gown
& sit with you while life
Elsewhere awaits me—& my dawn
Will be a morning's grief

I keep for keeping to myself
The secret pleasures of
These streets—if I spend my blood's wealth
On dope, & if I have

A little opium or rum,
& love the lure of strange
Men, while he waits for me at home,
With children, on a binge

Of priggish sorrows, crooked, bent
With expectations, so
Sick with discontent he can't
Call up one breath of joy—

If I decide this, who's to say
That I transgressed, or took
More than my equal share. As you
Sit lighting up that smoke

The match illuminates the smooth
Curve of your jaw. Sighs bloom.
It's livable here, now. I love
You, sir. Tell me your name.

Two Handwritten Pages

I. THOMAS JEFFERSON WRITES THE WORDS
"ALL MEN ARE CREATED EQUAL"

The room is small—almost austere.
A fire smolders in the grate
And makes a gloom of shadows here.
They lengthen with the hour. It's late.

He's not alone. Somewhere about
There's company that men who own
Men never are too long without,
The kind who know them to the bone.

He's fed and served by someone dark
As these twin shadows cast upon
The wall. Dark ink applied in stark,
Contrasting strokes. Stifling a yawn,

He gives a sigh, and seems to fret.
Perhaps the chair squeaks with his weight.
The other's quiet as a pet,
So Jefferson may concentrate.

The world's asleep. He's writing lines
His countrymen will carry down
The generations. He defines,
In this defiance of the crown

Of England, his own Time's best thought.
The quill makes scratching sounds, and draws
The words across the page. His bought
Black man attends to every pause.

(There are small chores to do, that keep
A bought man busy, keep him late

And occupied, in need of sleep.)
The silence in that room is Fate.

Two men, in their own way, proceed
As they have learned to do. The night
Wears thin. The written words will lead
To others, leading on to light.

Because that scribbled document
Is so abstract, it will be seen
One day as having surely meant
Exactly what it seems to mean.

2. LINCOLN WRITES THE
EMANCIPATION PROCLAMATION

Pennsylvania Avenue
Is wheel-rutted mud & hay & horses,
& leads on to the half-constructed
Capitol dome. McClellan's forces

Are letting Lee escape again,
A few miles up the dark, warm river.
Washington's a town they built
Out of a swamp, so there's the shiver

Of malarial summer all around,
The chill of fever in the campsites
Where men are dying not from war
But from the waiting. Damp nights

& killing inactivity,
& boredom, & great sickness for going
Home. Sharpsburg makes some hopeful news
Though. The ranged campfires are glowing.

Abe Lincoln sits behind his desk,
& sighs. Such deep emaciation,
All pangs, and his personal pain
Recedes in gloomy concentration—

He's decided that the time is right
For a provisional & partial
Change in the awful status quo—
An act less principled than martial.

In the quiet candlelight
He works, prepares his act of war.
A stratagem, to hurt the South.
But he's aware of something more:

What this will mean on history's
Stage. Europe's kings wait skeptically
For him to fail. He writes the line
Which ends in that one word: *Free.*

It will stir the populations, &
The world's chains will bend & sever.
A good man's melancholy mind
Articulates the change, forever.

Poem for Falstaff at the End

Oh, give me men of excess,
Round, rude men full of ale
& crumbs, Dry Sack & wine,
  who would spoil the even tenor
Of a country dinner, spouting
Jokes, singing bawdy songs.

Wings of angels in the voice
But the voice of fornication
& appetite, the happy passages
  giving over to the slightest
Temptation of the belly or the groin.
Such men are made for natural

Sport & are the best
Audience for a prince
Awaiting the cares of state
  & power, the indistinct
Vapors of intrigue, the ominous
Schemes, the machinations of the court.

Give me men who would teach
A prince how to be young
& careless, not like a king
  in anything—until the load
Of duty rests on the unkind,
Youthful shoulders & the new-made

King makes this very man
Dance a mortal dance for good—
  this corpulent clown who
  showed the fault
& bribery of flesh, the suck
Of living utterly for meat,

Solely for the rioting
& falling down, in the hours
When the parishioners lie abed,
        dreaming of night,
Dreaming of wandering in pools
Of dark, reeling with pleasures.

Here is this shaken creation,
Falstaff shivering the last,
Unable to believe it even
        as it happens—
A man who liked life instant
By instant & lived solely

For laughter & failure.
The one in whose rough,
Ruddy face my face shows,
        so much more
Closely similar to that coarse mask
Than to the visage of a king.

Movies

Imagine the stories of the minor characters in movies,
or envision major characters elsewhere . . .
—GEORGE GARRETT, in conversation

1. EARLY NURSE RATCHED

Fresh new Mildred on her first working day
Brought with her a small flower in a pot
And placed it lovingly in a safe spot:
A shelf above her desk, out of the way—

A pink tulip. Her uniform was crisp
With starch and clean as church. It gave, of course,
No hint of what she liked, nor of the force
With which she might one day correct a lisp

Or any inconsistence. She was young
And bright and wanted so to help all men.
She loved the mental ward the best. Back then
They used electric shock to loose the tongue.

They called it "treatment." She arrived at dawn.
She liked Muzak and violins so soft—
The sweetest notes, that seemed to drift aloft
& then you heard them drop like pennies on

Your soul. But on that fresh first day, so full
Of hope—with her name, Ratched, on her chest—
& her plans to help Man & all the rest,
You'd never have supposed her capable

Of murder. Would you? That smooth girl, so bright,
So certain of herself, so strong & good,
Holding her flower with its upturned hood
& her family picture (she's third from right—

Smiling that smile that drove us all cuckoo):
You'd never dream that little girl could kill
With just the tantrum strength of a child's will.
The girl she'd been was in the woman, too.

2. Mammy

In her dark dress she glides soft
Across the clear shine of the floor.
An upside-down reflection of her
Trails along wherever she goes.

In this mirrored version she seems
So elongated, that her great weight
Has no earthly consequence:
If she lifted away from the floor

She'd lift all the way to the top
Of the chandeliered central hall
Where she stands, waiting for him
To notice the red petticoats

He bought for her at great expense,
In Charleston. He will, & she'll make
A shy face with her deep brown eyes.
A comic moment. This man

& the former slave. He's entertained. She
Sleeps, he thinks, in the simple peace
Of the animals. She has lived with knowledge
She could be sold—& habitually performs feats

Of great intricacy, balancing
Her dignity & the old complacent idea

Of her, & hiding the fact that
She dreams of lovers, children, blood,

Flames, sex, death, the loss of heaven,
& the coming retribution—
& these are her waking dreams. She
Herself rejects them, fears them so.

For the appalling matter of this
Her life, here, in the city of
The time & place, is that she can't
Unthink fifty-five years of days

She's spent as who she sometimes
Is merely to survive. And worse, that
In the habit of performance
She half believes what he believes.

3. SAM

She says, "Play the song for me,
Sam." He hesitates, then plays
The goddamned thing. That's how
He thinks of it, now, bringing forth
The shaky notes on the old piano.

He's tired of it all. Tired of the boss
& his broken romance. But when Rick
Wants to talk, Sam will let him—
Sam's been with Rick for many years.
All the way to Casablanca.

He knows their story. He has no story.
He's just the piano player, background
Music in the bar Rick owns, and this
Is Rick's story. They're friends, you might
Say. But Sam calls him Mr. Rick.

Mr. Rick, alone with another kind
Of friend, given the place & time,
Might be heard to say that Sam's
A good darkie. Always was. A great
Companion and can he tickle

The ivory. He's got jazz in his blood,
Blues from Darktown, the hot saxes
& clarinets of New Orleans nights.
But Sam's never been near the city
Of New Orleans. We're in this city

In Africa, during the War against
The Germans & the Vichy French.
Sacrifice is necessary.
War brings out the best & worst,
As we all know, in men & women.

Sam goes home & finds himself
Unable to keep from tormenting
The young dark girl he lives with,
An Algerian whose parents
Died in the fall of Paris.

"Get away," he tells her. "What
Do you want me to do—you want
Me to sing a fucking song? Is that
It? You want some song & dance?
Fuck!" They met in El Alamein,
When Rick was on the run
From the heartbreak of Paris.

Her name is not important.
They once made love, trembling, under
The bright Moroccan moon, and he
Thought he had found the one thing,
The one answer for that long sorrow
Of the world as it had looked at him

And at him, all his life. The dead,
Blank objectifying gaze
That fixed him in its easy assumptions,
& snuffed his breathing & his past,
His every personal pang,

As if it were all no more than weather
In a foreign country. Even Rick,
In his cups, miserable, complaining
How, of all places, *she* would choose this one
Place, this bar to wander into.

Sam, playing desultorily the soft notes,
Recalls the morning, his own morning,
And the wrangling about German murderers,
& world's end, his general rage, which he's
Unable to control. He's wept in her arms,

Begging forgiveness. He's pleaded
With her to understand, & held her
So close that the faintly olive fragrance
Of her skin has stopped his breath.

But he never mentions this. Quiet,
Playing the notes with an automatic
Sweetness, he lets the boss go on
Drinking in his dreamy despair.
He plays the notes because he can.

He can manage them. He can always
Manage this. Even with the one
Key out of tune, the one dead string.

V   *Prose:* THOSE YEARS

So Long Ago

Indulge me, a moment.

I have often said glibly that the thing that separates the young from the old is the knowledge of what Time really is: not just how fast, but how illusive and arbitrary and mutable it is. When you are twenty, the idea of twenty years is only barely conceivable, and since that amount of time makes up your whole life, it seems an enormous thing—a vast, roomy expanse, going on into indefiniteness. You arrive at forty with a sense of the error in this way of seeing, and maturity, um, can be said to have set in.

And the truest element of this aspect of real time, of course, is the sense of the nearness of time past.

I have a memory of being bathed by my father on my seventh birthday. Morning, rainy light at a window. The swish and wash of lukewarm water. My own body, soft-feeling and small under the solid strong hands, lathered with soap. I said, "Well, I guess I'm a big boy now."

He said, "No, not quite."

I remember feeling a bit surprised, perhaps even downcast, that he didn't simply agree with me, as most of the adults in our large family usually did. He ran the towel over me, ruffled my hair with it, drying me off. I went across the hall into my room and dressed for the April day. Baseball season was starting.

Let me go back there for a little while, to that bath, my seventh birthday. At the time, I wasn't old enough to understand the difference between the humoring of children, which is a large part of any talk with them, and truth-telling, which is what my father did. I loved his rough hands on me, and the smell of him—aftershave, and cigarettes, and sometimes the redolence of my mother's perfume.

He hated lies, and lying. He was a storyteller, and he must have learned early how to exaggerate and heighten things, to make the telling go better, to entertain and enthrall. He was so good at it. He could spin it out and do all the voices and set the scene and take you to the laughs, and there simply *had* to have been elements that he fabricated. And yet he hated lies. Any trouble you ever got into in our house always had to do with that: you learned very early that even if you *had* done something wrong, something for which you wanted some kind of an excuse, or explanation, it had better not involve telling a lie.

I was often in some kind of mischief at school—my twin, Robert, and I had a talent for making other kids laugh, and for imitating our teachers' gestures and voice mannerisms. Well, we were the sons of a storyteller. Neither of us liked school very much; and the teachers, the nuns of Saint Bernadette's, knew it. They kept tabs on us. They were at some pains to discipline us. And whenever we got into a scrape at school, we lived in dread that our father would ask us, that evening, how things had gone at school. I remember sitting at the dinner table as he and my mother told stories, or commented happily on the various people—friends and family—who inhabited our lives then. Bobby and I would sit there in awful anticipation of the question: "How was school today?" You couldn't gloss over anything—you couldn't use a coverall word like "fine." You had to be specific, and you had to tell it all, the truth. You were *compelled* to do so by what you knew of the value he set upon the truth. And never mind philosophical truth, or the truth of experience, really; he wanted to know what happened in the day, what was said and done, and how it went—*that* kind of truth.

I have no memory—not even a glimmer—of how and when we learned that this was what he expected from us, and that the surest way to earn his displeasure was by lying to him. I don't have much of a memory of him telling us this; I recall him talking about how it was a thing *his* father expected, but by then I was in my teens, and I understood it then as an echo of a kind, a source.

All right.

I remember being surprised that in my father's truthful opinion I was not a big boy yet. I remember that we had two boys our age living next door to us, and that this took place on Kenross Avenue in Montgomery County, Maryland. I know intellectually that the year was 1952, and that Truman was still president. I could not have said who Truman was then, and I recall that a few months later, in the summer, when the Republican Convention was on our little General Electric black-and-white television, I saw all those people in the arena, with Eisenhower standing there on the podium, and I guessed the number to be everyone in the world. "No," my father said, "It's not even a small fraction of the number." I didn't know the word *fraction* and yet I understood what he meant.

Sometime around then I saw film of the war that had just ended, and I was told by my mother that another war was going on, in Korea. A summer evening—we were driving past an army post, and I had seen the anti-aircraft guns, the olive drab barrels aimed at the sky. I wondered aloud why we couldn't hear the guns.

"It's on the other side of the world, honey. Thousands of miles away."

In 1952, my mother was thirty-four years old. Now, I'm thirty years older than that, and this is the math I'm always doing—have been doing, like a kind of mental nerve-tic, since I was twenty-seven years old, and a father for the first time myself.

When my son Wes was fourteen months old, we moved to Iowa, where I attended the Writers' Workshop. I spent a lot of time with him that year, and as he grew slightly older I decided to conduct a sort of experiment: I'd see if I could manage to keep in his memory the times we had at Iowa—the swing set and sandbox outside the Hawkeye Court apartments, the little amusement park by the river in Iowa City, with its Ferris wheel and its kiddie train. I'd ask him about it, almost daily: "Do you remember the swing set? The sandbox? Do you remember how I used to push you on the swings, and you didn't want to go in the house? Remember the summer nights when it would be getting dark, and we'd go to that park and ride in the kiddie train?" Yes, he remembered. He was three, and then four, and then five, and he remembered. He offered elements of that time, so he wasn't merely remembering *my* memory: yes, the swing set and the sandbox—but did I remember the red wagon that got stuck there, and then buried there by the other children? I did. Yes, the kiddie train, but remember the buffalo? Yes, there had been a small enclosure with bison standing in it; the big Ferris wheel, yes, but did I remember riding it and being stopped at the very top?

Oh, yes.

I had begun to think I might be able to help my son carry that part of his life with him into his own adulthood—earliest memories that have chronological shape. It became important that he have it all to keep. And then one winter evening, as we were riding in the car on the way to a movie, I asked him about Iowa again, and he recalled nothing—it was all simply gone. I asked him about the swing set, the sandbox, the park, the train, the Ferris wheel, even the buffalo. To each one he said, "No." Innocently, simply, without the slightest trace of perplexity or anything of what I was feeling, which was sorrow. You could see him striving to get something of it back, but it was like a game, and there was nothing. No, he had no recollection of any of it. I don't think it had been more than a week or two since we had gone through this little litany of memory, and even so it had all disappeared from his mind, and my description of it was only a story, now.

When I was fifteen, my great-grandmother, Minnie Roddy, died. Minnie had raised my mother, because Minnie's daughter had had to go to work for the government when my mother was still a baby. They all lived with my Aunt Daisy, Minnie's sister, in a big, sprawling Victorian house with a wide porch that had blue-gray painted boards and white trim. When Minnie began to fail, my mother went over there, and we later learned, through the talk of the adults in the rooms of the two houses, that she was holding the old woman in her arms in the last moments. Minnie used to tell me stories, sitting in the breakfast nook, by the windows where younger children ran. Summer evenings, the cousins and aunts and uncles out on the lawn, throwing horseshoes. The bell-like clang of the metal on metal when someone hit one of the posts, or scored a ringer or a leaner. Fireflies rising in the shallow pools of shade in the spaces between the houses, in the cloud-shaped willow tree—you couldn't see its trunk for the drooping filamental mass of its branches—at the edge of the property. Minnie talking, telling me about coming from Ireland on a ship; about her husband—who had come to America after killing a man in a fight one afternoon in a pub in Dublin. Her voice would trail off, and the louder voices out the window would distract me. I'd nod and pretend to listen. I was always reading books, as Bobby was, but it showed more on me, and I was the one, after all, who believed that I had a vocation. I was planning for the priesthood. Minnie Roddy would say, "You'll grow up and tell these stories. You'll grow up and be a writer."

And she would go on talking, unscrolling her memory of earlier days, of my mother as a young girl; of Ireland, and a childhood spent, for the most part, in the latter part of the nineteenth century. I didn't hear most of it. I nodded and pretended to listen, while this woman—this tiny slip of a lady with her wire-framed glasses and her clear large blue eyes—tried to give me treasure, something to store up, for the arrival of a season I was not and am not ready for.

When she died, it was decided that Bobby and I were old enough to attend the funeral. I felt a strange detached curiosity about the whole thing: I was actually going to see a dead person. I told one of the other boys in my class, speaking it out with a sort of quiet, fake-brave shrug. "I'm going to see a dead person today."

"Who?"

"My great-grandmother."

"Jesus, no kidding?"

I was, I suppose, even a little proud of the fact. Minnie had lived to a great age, and her going seemed natural enough, and so far away from my own life and world that I could only think of it in a sort of abstract haze. I was still young enough and egocentric enough to be unable quite to imagine my own demise.

The day of the funeral was bright and chilly. I don't recall whether it was spring or fall. It wasn't summer, because I was in school. I think it was fall. We rode with our parents to the funeral home, and I was like a secret traveler in the back seat, planning my exploration of this curiosity, death, this unreal element of the life I was in so permanently. I was wildly curious; I understood, according to the tenets of the faith I had been raised in, that Minnie Roddy would not be there, but only her body, the empty vessel she had vacated. She was in that blue elsewhere that I associated with the sky, and we could now pray to her.

Blue is the important color, here.

Standing over the box where she lay, looking like a bad likeness of herself, I saw the forking, colorless veins in her bony hands, the fingers of which were wound with a black rosary; and I saw the blue place at her earlobe, where blue did not belong. I marked it, and knew that I would never forget it.

This sounds as though I were marking things with the flaccid, nervous sensitivity of one of those pretentious people who like to think of themselves as a romantic central figure in their own drama: the incipient artist, observing everything with an eye to later recording it. I do not mean it this way at all, and it was not like that at all. I was a child, still. I knew next to nothing about anything, especially about myself. And I don't know that I have learned much since then, either.

I suppose I have to admit that it might just be impossible to have it both ways: to claim that I was not that hypersensitive romantic figure, the artist-as-a-young man, and still report the impressions of a moment like that one, standing over the body of a woman who had lived a life so separate from mine, and nothing like mine, and whose reality could not have anticipated that she would be a figure in my speech, a character in a story I would tell, even as she told me about all the living she had seen and done, and I pretended to listen. In any case, I do not mean this the way it will sound. I mean to express the quality of a memory, in order to say something about this life we live, so much of which is fugitive, so much of which is lost in the living of it.

The room we were in was banked with flowers, and there were chairs in rows, as though someone might give a lecture, or a homily. Minnie's coffin looked to have been where it was long enough for this prodigious wall of flowers to grow up on three sides of it. There was a dim light, a candle burning at one end. The light was brightest where she lay, with her eyes shut in a way that made you understand they would not open again. The skin looked oddly transparent, like the synthetic skin of a doll. And there was the blue place at the ear, the place, I knew, where the cosmetics of the mortician hadn't quite taken. I stood there and looked with a kind of detached though respectful silence at this, aware of it not as death, quite, but death's signature. I was conscious of the difference. I spent my minute there, head bowed, and then walked back to my seat at the rear of the room with the other young people, all in their early teens, like me. I saw my mother and my Aunt Florence come from where I had just been, and my mother had a handkerchief that she held to her nose. She sobbed, once. Earlier, when we had arrived, Florence had come up to my mother and said, "You scared the be-Jesus out of me." I don't know—or I don't remember—what this was about; I think it had something to do with what had gone on last night, at the viewing. Perhaps my mother had gotten woozy, or swooned. It was the first time I had ever heard the phrase *be-Jesus*.

Florence and my mother sat down, and a priest led us in the rosary. If he said anything about the woman who lay behind him in the long box, I don't recall it. We were in the room for a time, and then people began to file out. I remained in my seat, and I have no idea why. Others crossed in front of me, and maybe I was saying my own prayers—it seems to me now that I must've felt some pang of guilt for my oddly remote observation of everything, and was trying to say the words of a prayer, repeating them inwardly in an attempt to say them not out of automatic memory but actually to enter into the meaning of them:

Hail Mary, full of grace,
the Lord is with thee.
Blessed art thou among women,
and blessed is the fruit of thy womb, Jesus.

Holy Mary, Mother of God,
pray for us sinners,
now and at the hour of our death. Amen.

The others were all filing quietly out of the long room, and I saw the mortician step to the side of the casket, where we had each stood only moments before. With a practical sureness, the nearly offhand familiarity of experience, he reached into the white satin that ringed Minnie Roddy's head, and pushed downward on it, a tucking motion, and Minnie slipped from her sleeping pose. Her head dropped down into that box like a stone.

Something must have shown in my face; and the mortician's wife—let us call them the Hallorans, because I no longer recall the name—saw the change in my features. Later, as I was getting into the back of my father's car, Aunt Florence leaned in and said, ' Honey, Mrs. Halloran wanted me to tell you that Mr. Halloran was only making it so Minnie could rest better."

I nodded. I don't believe I said anything. It was almost as if I had stumbled upon someone in a privy act; I felt the same kind of embarrassment. But there was something else in it, too, a kind of species-thrill: this was the human end, a reality I was not expecting. I am trying to express this as exactly as I can, and of course it is finally inexpressible. I know that all my fascination was gone, and I sat there in the back of the car, looking out at the sunny streets of Washington, and felt numb, far down.

That memory is as present to me as the moment, almost a decade earlier, when I said to my father that I was a big boy, and he told me the truth, that I was not a big boy. Not yet. Those memories are as near as the memory of asking, in the first line of this story, for your indulgence.

Of course, this is not an original perception; yet one arrives at it in life—doesn't one?—with the sense of having had a revelation: one's personal past is a *place,* and everything that resides there does so in contemporaneous time. What, then, of the collective past? The collective memory? That is where chronology really is. We come from the chaos of ourselves to the world, and we yearn to know what happened to all the others who came before us. So we impose Time on the flow of events, and call it history. For me, Memory is always *story.* True memory is nothing like the organized surface of a story, yet that is all we have to tell it, and know it, and experience it again: but if we are doomed to put our remembered life into stories, we are blessed by it, too.

I never spoke to my mother and father, or even to my brothers and sisters, about what I had seen at the funeral home. I don't know why, now. I can't recall why. Perhaps it was too private, finally; and perhaps I did not want to have it in memory, didn't want to fix it there in the telling. But it has never left me. It is with all the others, large and small, important and meaningless, all waiting in the same timeless dark, to drift toward the surface when I write, or daydream, or sleep.

The Porch
1961

WE ARRIVE IN AN UPROAR of summer voices, piling out of our new Ford,
with its tail fins that are smaller than last year's, and its wraparound wind-
shield. Our father sells cars, now—has done so since late 1957, when he left
his job with the Agriculture Department against the advice of his parents
and almost everyone else he knew—and we have grown accustomed to having
the latest models to ride around in. There are six of us—the girls, Barbara
and Betty, eighteen and fourteen respectively; the twins, Bobby and me,
sixteen only two months ago; and the babies, as we call them—Tim, who is
six, and Steve, who is ten.

The babies are too young to understand what this visit is really all about.
We have come to my mother's family home in Washington, D.C., a big Vic-
torian house on a shady street near Catholic University. Cousins and aunts
and uncles greet us from the wide lawn, with its big, overspreading trees,
its continents of brightness and shade. Barbara, a young woman now, leads
the babies through everyone, accepting the kisses and the teasings. Bobby
follows them, with his hands in his pockets and his head down; he's a pool
shark. Very cool. The aunts and uncles call him "the bad one," meaning it
as a joke, and of course, being sixteen, he has taken it deeply, and with pain,
to heart. He wears pointy-toed Italian shoes and tight peg-legged pants;
a white shirt and a dark vest. His dark red hair is combed high, and then
pulled down in the center of his forehead. He walks around the side of the
big house to the long backyard, where the men are throwing horseshoes.
I watch him go. I'm a basketball player—quite good at it, in fact. We are
identical twins, but we do not have a lot to say to each other these days; even
our friends are different. I wear white slacks, a blue shirt with the sleeves
rolled up. My hair is combed something like Ricky Nelson's. I'm devout,
and bookish (Bobby is also bookish, but he hides it better), and everyone
knows I'm planning for the priesthood. I'm "the good one," which I have
also taken to heart, though without being quite conscious of it. Bob and
Helen are our parents—in their young forties, with a big family growing up
on them, and more money than they are accustomed to having. They are
in love, after almost twenty years of marriage, and they know it.

Together, they walk across the wide lawn to the house, carrying gifts. This
is Minnie Roddy's eightieth birthday. Helen is Minnie's granddaughter.

Helen's father died in the great flu epidemic of 1918, and she never knew him. Her mother, Louise, had to go to work for the District, as the adults put it, meaning Washington. So Minnie Roddy and her sister, Daisy, brought Helen up, and after Louise married Dick Underwood, and little Florence came along, they brought her up, too. Dick Underwood is a man with a tendency to let the bottle get the best of him; he is always going and coming, in and out of the family's good graces. By 1961, it has been several years since I've seen him; I remember that he had a big car, and thousands of books. Even more than the many at our own house in the suburbs, twenty minutes away.

One lost summer day when Bobby and I were very small, he pulled up in front of the house in the big car and asked us if we wanted to go for a little ride. It was a big tan convertible, and the top was down. The shine on it gave us back ourselves as sharply as if we had been gazing in a beige mirror. We climbed in, excited and happy, and very impressed with him, and with a laugh deep in his throat he swung out into the road. We felt the cool breeze moving over us, and we looked at the brightly polished dashboard with all its interesting dials and buttons and vents. He drove past the anti-aircraft guns of Fort Myer, and on out into the Virginia countryside. He let us stand and face into the wind. At one point, he said, "Guess we better get on back, because I've got to wee." We laughed helplessly at this, since we had never heard an adult use the word. When we pulled in front of the house, perhaps half an hour later, Helen came out into the front yard and chased him away. "Don't you ever come back here," she shouted.

Later, Helen learned from her mother, Louise, that he came back home and walked up onto the porch and began to cry. "That daughter of yours doesn't like me much." We were not told any of this at the time, of course.

At sixteen I know it, though, as I know that Louise has recently suffered a kind of breakdown. I am grown up enough to have gleaned this knowledge, even as my parents have been fairly close-mouthed about it. I am aware of this gathering of the family as a celebration, but also as a means to offer support and comfort to one of its number. That one is seated in the porch swing now, looking like herself to me, as I climb the steps of the porch.

"Come here," she says, reaching for me. She is dark, with deep-socketed eyes, and prominent cheekbones. There are photographs in the foyer of this big house that show how beautiful she was in 1921, and '31, and '41. Her arms are thinner than I recall, and her voice is a note lower, it seems.

She puts her arms around me, and I pat her bony shoulders. Next to her in the swing is Aunt Daisy. Eighty-four, big-shouldered, with heavy arms and spotted skin, and the rounded features of some other branch of the Roddy clan, she is a kindly woman with a strange bluntness about her. Her directness is something I try to avoid always, and am seldom able to.

Now she says, "Louise, let someone else get a hug."

Louise lets go of me. I walk into Aunt Daisy's heavy arms. "When you gonna get some meat on those bones?" she says.

This has become a favorite question of hers these days, and of course I have no answer to it. "I don't know," I say. The universal childhood dodge, and I feel vaguely resentful for having been drawn into it: I want to think of myself as an adult now. I am old enough to drive a car, and my father occasionally lets me have a glass of beer. I smoke—though they do not know this yet.

"You're a good boy," Louise says, patting my shoulders as if to test the muscles. "Nice broad shoulders. I have such handsome grandchildren."

"He's too skinny, if you ask me," says Aunt Daisy.

Louise says, "No one asked you."

"I said if you did," Aunt Daisy says.

I step back and let the others greet her and Louise—who wants to know where the babies are. Somewhere nearby, I hear the sound of baseball being announced on a radio. The Senators are playing the hated Yankees, and Roger Maris has just hit another home run; he's far ahead of Ruth's pace, and is leaving Mantle behind, too. Now and again, there's the clang of the horseshoes hitting the iron stake out back. Someone shouts my older sister's name. "Barbara, Barbara."

"Where's Minnie?" my mother asks.

"Inside," says Aunt Daisy. "She baked some things for the children."

The wind moves the shade on the grass here in front of the house, where two cousins are lobbing a ball back and forth. I want to take part in this, yet I'm also now interested in what's being said between my father and Louise. His tone is almost the same as the one he uses with us when he means to discipline us. "You're never as alone as you think you are, Weezy. You ought to try remembering that."

"I couldn't feel it," Louise says. "Couldn't feel a thing."

"But you know it. Don't you. We're all with you, everywhere you go. Why don't you pick up the phone and call somebody."

"Couldn't make myself do anything."

"She needs a good rest," Aunt Daisy says.

Louise says, "Not that kind of rest, Daisy."

"Don't put words in my mouth."

"Not everything has to do with working too hard—that's all I meant. Rest doesn't solve everything. It has nothing to do with loneliness, for instance."

"Well, we're all here now," says my father. "No reason for anybody to feel alone."

"You feel whatever comes," Louise says. "Or whatever refuses to come." Her voice is calm, almost casual. She looks right at me, and I am oddly aware that there are angles of bone in her face that are like my mother's, and mine. For some reason, I think of death, of the dark Irish I heard Uncle Charles talking about one afternoon earlier in this summer, when the first inklings of the trouble came through to me. I have been thinking a lot of death, too, lately. And abruptly, I sense some stream of propensity flowing into me from this thin, nervous woman with her shadowed eyes. At the time, of course, I am unable to express this feeling, even to myself. I have no words; only the slight chill of recognizing my own face in her face. I go down off the porch and out into an afternoon of games—tag, baseball, horseshoes.

Toward evening, I go up on the porch again, and stand gazing out at the ramshackle, flat-roofed building across the street. Clumps of grass have pushed up through the blue gravel in front of it, and a slab of concrete looks as though it's crumbling away into the weeds just beyond the side door. I have no idea what this building is (perhaps it was once a gas station?), but it interests me, since it is so clearly abandoned, empty. Beyond it, on a raised and well-kept bed of darker-blue gravel, is a railroad track. I have been told many times that I am not to go over there, but I am sixteen now, and I figure that I've reached the age of being able to decide for myself. I know that sooner or later all the adults will go inside, and there will be a window of opportunity, a chance to go over and put my hands down on the cold iron, and think of the train. I might even get to see the train, though in all the times I have been to this house, I have no memory of ever seeing one.

So I wait on the porch, and the adults do go inside, my grandmother leaning on my father's arm. Everyone, that is, except Aunt Daisy, who sits in the swing and moves just enough to make the chains squeak. I'm only partially aware of the sound, standing with my bony elbows on the railing, gazing out across the shade and sun.

"What're you day-dreaming about?" Aunt Daisy asks me.

I turn to look at her. She's at the other end of the porch; a distance. The wide, shaded expanse seems momentarily to shift, as though I have faltered at the perception of its size. "I was hoping to see a train go by," I say.

She glances out at the street, her street. She has lived here for thirty years. She nods. "They come by at night, and very early in the morning."

"I don't think I've seen one come by."

"You just don't remember. We had to go over there and get your brother and you one time. You were both sitting on the bank on the other side of the track, up high in those weeds, and when the train came through it stopped, and you were stuck there. You both started crying. The whole street heard the noise you two made."

I strain to remember this, and can't.

"You don't remember."

"No ma'am," I say.

"What're you going to do with yourself?"

"Ma'am?" I say.

"You're almost grown. You going to be an artist, like your mother?"

Aunt Daisy has seen my drawings, and it is only recently that I have been informed that the pastels on the living room wall—of Christ in the garden, of people in a rainy street—are Helen's work, done while she was still in high school. They are all so much better than my own, so much more complete; startlingly exact and true to life. There are more of them in the piano bench, and in various places about the house—something they have all taken for granted. Helen herself merely smiles at the plain astonishment of her children at this thing she has done better than any of them, without ever letting them know when she appreciated their meager efforts just how far from her own drawings they are.

"Well?" Aunt Daisy says.

"I don't know," I say. "I guess so."

We're quiet. In a few moments, the big tan convertible pulls up, years older but just as waxed and polished and new-looking, and Dick Underwood gets out. He comes across the lawn, looking very natty, in two-tone shoes and a beige three-piece suit. He's smoking a cigar.

"Daisy," he says, coming up onto the porch.

"When you gonna quit that smelly cigar," Daisy says.

"Sometime," he tells her. He looks at me. "Hey, boy."

At the door, Louise's Uncle Charles, with his own cigar, says, "Well, you made it after all."

"Charley."

The screen door opens, and Dick Underwood goes on inside. I hear my mother greet him in the foyer of the house, as everyone else does. "Helen," he says distinctly over the voices of the others. "Where's the birthday girl?"

"In the kitchen," my mother says.

I hear him wish Minnie Roddy a happy birthday. And I hear him ask Louise how she is feeling.

"Sometimes," Aunt Daisy says to me, "the trains don't come for days. It's just a switching track now, I think."

"A what?"

She gets up from the swing and walks to me, slow, in her odd, thick-heeled shoes. She takes my elbow and leads me to the edge of the stairs, and points at the tracks. "They use it to switch cars. They come part way, then go back—part way and back, that's all. It has something to do with the station, which is over there. But up on that side of the track, that hill over there, is where you and your brother were."

I follow her hand with my eyes, and even amid the noise and confusion coming from the rooms behind us her gesture seems to promise some tranquilizing effect on everything, as if she has raised her hand to ask for quiet from the world. And indeed it all does seem to pause. And in that pause I receive a visceral sense of how it is in life—I will never be able to explain this any more directly than to say that in that moment I am aware that there is trouble, and that somehow in this casual gesture of Aunt Daisy's, showing me where I once was separated from this house by the huge noise and clatter of a train, she gives me the strongest bodily impression of where the rest of the world leaves off and we begin.

"You see?" she says. "Do you remember now?"

I do not. Yet the feeling that where we are standing is the edge of our world has stopped my breath.

"Son?" she says.

"Yes ma'am," I say.

A little later, I'm sitting on the top step, with a palm full of salt. The dinner has been served—hamburgers and hot dogs from the barbecue in back, potato salad, and baked beans; deviled eggs, ambrosia fruit salad, biscuits. The men are playing horseshoes in back, and are letting Bobby play with them. He's holding his own. I'm eating the salt, dipping my wet index finger into it, and then putting the finger in my mouth. I have had part of a glass of beer, and have experienced something of the frustration of being too old to sit with the babies and too young to sit with the adults. I have argued with Bobby about the train—he claims to remember quite well the incident of being caught on the other side of the thing—and I'm filled with fear because, in the casual conversation over dinner, my mother has mentioned that she had the tumor on her neck looked at.

We were all in the big lighted kitchen, sitting around the white table when she said it, talking to her half sister, Florence. "It's nothing," she said, "but a cyst."

"Are you going to have it removed?" Florence asked.

"We'll see. He said it was up to me."

"I think you should get it removed," said their mother, who sat with her hands folded on the table top, like someone waiting for a meeting to begin. She hadn't touched her food. And the conversation quickly shifted to attempts at getting her to eat.

"You don't eat enough to keep alive," Florence said.

And my father made a joke. "Guess we'll have to spoon it down you, Weezy, like we just stopped doing with the babies."

"I'll eat, if everyone will stop watching me," Louise said.

A little later, crouched in the side yard with the cousins, I heard Peggy, the oldest cousin at nineteen, tell of an auto accident a friend of hers witnessed. "There was a man in the car, all crunched up and barely breathing and they worked for hours to get him out. The windshield was all smashed out and then somebody found a pair of shoes on the passenger side, and they realized there'd been another person in the car. So they started looking for this other person, and a man comes walking down the street toward them, kind of staggering, just in socks, and every little vein in his skin is bursting with blood, but the skin itself isn't broken. He was bright, bright red, just under the surface of the skin, and of course he was walking dead. Died before they got him in the ambulance. Not one break in the skin, and not a drop of blood on the ground."

Now, sitting on the porch eating the salt, I am trying to stop being afraid, trying not to think about dying, or being so alone that you wanted to die; trying hard to trust my mother's casualness about the cyst. Minnie Roddy has come out and is in the swing, humming softly, fanning herself with part of the day's newspaper. She's got dark, metal-colored hair, kept close to her head by a net; she wears metal-framed glasses, small and square, and she looks like a slighter, more chiseled version of her daughter and granddaughter.

"You shouldn't eat salt like that," she says to me. "You'll get hardening of the arteries when you get older."

It seems to me that I have always understood the idea of growing older, though it nevertheless has always felt impossible, something so far away as to be unimaginable, or nearly so. It feels quite present to me now, sitting here with the salt in my palm, hearing the squeak of the swing where Minnie Roddy sits.

Other children come up on the porch, led by Peggie and her sister Bitsy. The light is changing, the sun having moved to the other side of the house, beyond the tall roof with its towering chimneys and gabled dormers. The coolest place is here, in the shade, looking out at the darker green of the lawn with the massive shadow of the house in it. Children run in and out, younger than I, and of no interest to me. The screen door slaps to in its wooden frame, and the games these children are engaged in look to me now like the social life of another species. I am thinking of the dark that is coming; cysts, mental troubles, troubles with the bottle; old age and death. I don't want any of it. I want to go back to being a child, knowing nothing.

Aunt Daisy comes to the screen door and calls to all those who want cookies and ice cream.

Minnie Roddy says my name from the swing.

"Yes, ma'am," I say.

She pats the slats at her side in the swing. "Sit with me."

The others are running in the side yard, and out in front, too. Hide and seek. The day's heat is diminishing slowly. She talks to me, telling me stories. She tells how Helen, walking down the hallway of Holy Cross High School at sixteen years of age, pinched the rear end of a cute, sandy-haired athlete who at that moment was talking to one of the nuns. The sandy-haired boy let out a shriek and startled the nun, who had no idea why a young man being told about his assignment having to do with King Lear should suddenly cry out like that. The young man was my father, of course, though Minnie doesn't say this; it's understood that I know. I laugh; I'm quite familiar with the story, but I love to hear it told. And then she begins talking of her husband, who left Ireland after killing a man in a fist fight in a pub. She has his picture, and I've seen it—a sharp-featured man with a shock of white hair and bushy white eyebrows, standing in bright sun, the eyes narrow, buried in a network of wrinkles. Minnie Roddy talks about when she met him, what she was wearing on that day in the last century, and her voice begins trailing off, as it has always done, as long as I have known her. I make an effort to listen, being polite, possessing no sense of her as having ever been anything but what she is: one of the old people; one of the stolid, warming presences of the house. She talks on, and soon my mother joins us, commenting about the cooling day, the fresh air, the good smell of the food. Others come out, Aunt Florence, Aunt Daisy, Uncle Charles, Dick Underwood, my father. My cousins Bitsy and Peggy; Aunt Marian and Uncle Francis, who made my father laugh against his will the first time they met and has been making him laugh ever since.

That first time was on this porch. An evening very much like this one. My father on a date with Helen, and Marian on a date with Francis. Minnie Roddy brought some small dishes of vanilla ice cream out for the young folks, and when she offered Francis's to him, he threw his arms up and made a sound of tremendous alarm and consternation, startling poor Minnie to the point of nearly falling backward into my father's lap. "What in the world is wrong with you, young man?" Minnie said.

And Francis, still in the voice of someone quite alarmed, said, "Madam, I'll have you know I didn't even eat that stuff when I was poor."

My father tells this story again, and everyone, including Minnie, laughs at it again. Francis claims it's not true, but no one steps up to support him in this, least of all Minnie Roddy, who smiles tolerantly at him from the swing. Standing in the light of the open door are Louise and Dick Underwood, looking quite comfortable together, an old couple. Louise laughs at something one of the babies says about the bathtub upstairs, that it looks like it has real feet.

"Those are called claw feet, aren't they?" she says.

"They're scary," Helen says. "I always thought so when I was small."

"Nothing ever scared you," says her mother. "You climbed on a streetcar when you were three. Just toddled right up and got on."

"It's all that red hair," Dick Underwood says. "All that fire."

"Well," Uncle Charles says. "It's time."

A man has been hired to take a photograph. It has been decided that before we all sing "Happy Birthday" to Minnie, we'll have the photo taken. We are in the process of arranging ourselves, smaller children on the top steps of the porch, teenagers on the next ones down, adults on the descending steps, according to height. The photographer busily orchestrates this, running back and forth, trying to be efficient while entertaining and reassuring the smaller children. At length, in all the noise and bustle, he manages to get several shots, and in the next moment—before he can get the camera off its tripod, the group has scattered to all parts of the house and grounds.

Dusk is coming fast. Fireflies flicker everywhere in what looks like a perpetual rising, cinders lifting out of an invisible conflagration. There's the sound of the porch swing, and of the screen door slamming, and Minnie Roddy's small voice, talking. We sing "Happy Birthday," and she opens her gifts with her bony, crooked fingers. I hear my mother's laugh above all the voices, and the fear closes in on me again. (This fear turns out to be groundless—and how strange, now, to think of it—the cyst is nothing more than that.) She's talking to Minnie about how she always loved to sit on this porch in the summer evenings, with everything so peaceful, and wait for my father to come walking down the street from one of his baseball games, still wearing his uniform, his glove hooked to his belt. All those wonderful times before the war.

"Happy birthday," she says to Minnie, and I can see that she's trying not to cry. But her face is all aglow in the light, and these are obviously tears of happiness. Some small element of this day has reassured her about her mother's trouble, and she is for the moment joyous, not dwelling on whatever else may be worrying her—the constant concern for her six children, and her husband, everyone in her large, boisterous family. She kisses Minnie on the cheek, then rises and says it's time to go. She asks me to help her gather everyone. I do. I'm the good one, remember. I fetch Bobby and the girls from the backyard, where they have been helping Bitsy catch fireflies; the babies are with Aunt Florence in the parlor, eating cookies. We all say our good-byes, kissing the aunts and uncles, and the cousins. Special care is taken that we all kiss Louise, who seems cheerful in a strangely hurried way, as if she's late for something, a little out of breath trying to catch up. Minnie Roddy, her mother, stands at her side, one hand on her shoulder. We wave at them all from the new car, and then my father pulls us all away, and on into the summer night. I look back from the new car window at the light on that porch, the people standing there waving good-bye.

That was forty-six years ago. Helen, in this memory, is more than seventeen years younger than I am now. In the coming years, several people who posed for that photograph on the steps of the porch, including Minnie Roddy and Grandmother Louise, will die in her arms—she being the one of all of us who manages somehow not to let fear stop her from what she sees needs doing. With all of them she is patient, loving, practical.

Once, when bathing her dying father-in-law, she is lifting him and he loses his bowels. "I'm sorry," he says. "Stop it," she tells him, quickly and efficiently cleaning it away. "Don't be silly.' She kisses him on the forehead. He thanks her, and again she tells him not to be silly.

Through the years, she will talk of death as though it is something one has to do, a task, no more momentous than any other unpleasant task, a thing to get through and be done with. She will go on to lose Barbara in an automobile accident—and her family, all her other children, will scatter to the four winds. Will change, with families of their own. In 1985 she herself goes to sleep forever, cradled by her husband of so many years, so many houses and rooms; so many seasons with their attendant losses and delights, excitements and falterings, and the steady courage, the audaciousness and bravery and excellence of long love, the love that allows for every change, and itself does not change.

The big old family home is gone now. I have stood on the street where it once was, and recognized the railroad track, which is still there. The apartment building which occupies the ground where the house stood is dilapidated looking, running to seed itself. Yet, standing on that street, for a fierce minute it is as if I can hear the voices of that summer afternoon and evening all those years ago, and I am once again standing on the steps of the porch with that feeling of being on a sort of promontory or precipice—that sense of the world out there, separate from this world here, with its familiar and so comfortably beloved sounds, even in the complication of fearing the changes I am just old enough to know are coming.

These decades later, I let the memory walk into me, through me. I greet it.

And I think of my own children, the porch where my children danced with my father, danced to the Benny Goodman music he so loved. And I think how, if the feeling is right and the love is as excellent and brave as it was when I was young, these children will carry the porch with them out into the harshness and turmoil of the world, and it will go on providing for them, even when they are far away, even when that house, too, is gone, and they have all come to see other places as the places they have for love, and shelter.

Oh, Welcome. Welcome.

VI GARDEN

Wild Forces Rave

In the coils of cloud
At the limit
Of this night sky: edges
Move like
Running children,
Shadows like fear.

I know the bottom
Of that & so do you.
We crouch in the lee of a wall.
Years crowd in, losses,
The fright-borne

Winds, dark as
Cave-corners, cruel
As stilled breath.

All will come
Back around to peace,
Though.

Love is indeed
Turbulent in all
Its facets: life-wild
As water, but it
Tends toward final
Calm—a face
Looking at you & saying
"Oh, good. Oh, yes.'

Trust this. My love,
The sky is mansions
Of freezing dark tonight,

But will end in soft,
Unutterably beautiful
Light at the eastern
Edges, in the cold.

That light will expand
& rise like a lazy sleeper
Over the blue curve
Of the world: but we
See a notion of sorrow
In this brightness.

& we follow it
Down.
          We have no choice
(Left to our own devices,
We would surely turn to clay).
But here, everything is a sign.
Everything points to love.

Our good countryside
Steams with it.
Rising breezes carry
The sighings of animals.
The world tends to forms
Of unity. That's us—
Morning edging over
The black folds of the sky.

Flying to Laramie, Wyoming

From thirty thousand feet, the land west and north
Of Denver looks like the surface of some other planet.
The patterns are circular. Big circles in rows—
I keep thinking of missile silos. I know they are all

There somewhere in the great expanse of mostly
Empty ground—mile upon mile of rucked,
Bunched earth, not-quite mountains and then mountains,
With strange black tips and areas that look burned.

The little aircraft shakes in the tumbling winds
Of the upper plains, the great plateau, as it is rightly
Called. There are highways, but they look like
Little cracks in the chapped side of a giant urn.

I can see the curving of the world away
Toward California and Washington and Oregon.
This little machine with its roaring propellers and
The twenty-four souls in it, heading far, traveling

Deeper into this young century. I feel strange,
Alone. There is an old woman in back, holding
Tight to her purse. I feel strange, I said. Alone. She
Keeps muttering something, her lips barely moving.

She gazes out the window and I wonder what
She sees, if she is going away or coming home.
And I want, more than anything, to go home—
To our home, where the girl is saying more words

Every day, and our happiness grows, our obdurate
And wonderful love increases in laughter and little
Whisperings across the pillow, awake and asleep,
My love. My complicated girl, my blood and life.

I love you. I say it, mutter my own prayer like
The old lady in the rearward seat. I love you. I am
An old man muttering on a plane, at thirty thousand
Feet, above a vast landscape of wilderness crossed

With the marks and scars of human striving as far
As the eye can see. I love you, I love you, this prayer
As we all hurtle toward a small strange city,
And the winds buffet us and we buck and dip.

I hold on to the thought of you—so joyous
Even in sadness—& our little lovely girl.
The far clouds look like cities made of stone.
You move in my chest like my very heart.

Garden

Next to the knowledge of death, the discovery of paradox is
                        what frightens most. We learn awfully
    that two things can be true and contradictory at the same time, exactly
at that age when we feel deeply
                the need for some vision that's free
of error, falsity, misconception. We crave the clearest water.
                    We seek the soft words.
    Whispers of love, a child's purest excitement, like an answer.
                    We seek the warm hand
on the shoulder, kindness,
                    mercy, even forgiveness.
                                    Living yields up confusion.
            As I, little one, lead you
                        into the garden, I see
time dissolve, as we say, like waves of heat
    on a blistering summer day—
                    oh, it does dissolve and confound.

        I was time-haunted. The shadows fell early each live-long day,
            and lay down like mortality on the soul.

                    My heart's garden was despair.

2

Solomon's Seal, Cherry Laurel, Yellow Bishop's Hat, American Snow Bell.
            Under the Memphis sun you walk, green hat shading your face
            and all around you are the shapes of the garden:
                Stokes' Aster, Adam's Needle, Fire Witch, Autumn Sage,
Caesar's Brother, Lamb's Ear.

        In the flower-fragrant shade, you're home. The world is far.

In the Middle Eastern deserts, killing goes on. And on: car bombs explode, children

        die. Families labeled
                as "next of kin" are notified. Notified. My God.
                        And as always the news is conflicting. But this is
                war. And beyond war,
a terrible randomness reigns
                      a calamity of forces trying to
            manage chaos. Families displaced by storms, fires, soldiers . . .

In the newspaper this morning there were the faces of children, crying.
            All the governments fail to manage. Travail, trials.
              Massacres, disruptions in the social fabric. Yet this garden

                  is green and chattering
            birds sail over the upturned heads of the flowers.

Iris, Lancelot Hosta, Slender Deutzia, Palace Purple Coral Bells

    3

This is how you are in the world. The darkness falters around you.
                        Horrors are beaten back.
        On the wide avenue of botanical wonders, you stroll,
appreciating everything with your best spirit,
            every leaf or petal or stalk, all the shapes & sizes.
        You visit with them, a friendly presence under the branches
            of the elm.

Magnolia, Chinaberry, Southern Oak, Bur Oak.

The shade welcomes you.

Golden Sedge, Palace Purple Coral Bells, Schilling's Dwarf, Evergreen Candytuft.

4

Oh, I have been the terrible migrations.
                I have been war. Now, along a sweetly cut path beneath poplar
                                and black gum & dogwood, I marvel
            every minute:
        how delicate are the veins in the leaves, how organized the deep
                yellow
blossoms are in the little pockets of sun.

                        American
Snow Bell, Bluestar, Yellow Bishop's Hat, Jet Trail Flowering Quince, Lemon Thyme.
        Variegated Sweet Flag.

5

I think about how, all around us, disarray waits, a stealthy watcher. Dream-slayer.
            The roads in the city give forth collisions and injuries,
                            angers, failures of sight. The streets are full
        of refuse and tossed trash. There are
                        chasms between spirits in the lonely rooms behind windows.

            I fear so for you
                        in the ruck and confusion of America, Dear!

Yet you move with such swaying grace, in this warm, sun-dappled light,
                    as day-lilies bend with breezes—the floral, soft air,
            like a scarf
                        traced lightly across our faces.
        Golden Sedge, Japanese Plum Yew, Painted Arum, Moonbeam, Sugar Hackberry.

        Entering a puddle of shade in the grass, you turn and smile,
    perfectly glad,
                floppy hat

cocked at a lovely angle.
Sirens wail beyond us
& the butterfly will
not quite hold still long enough to be photographed.

The Longing

Yesterday it rained & misted
& the trees waved in the wind.
But that changed.

As the afternoon arrived,
Sunlight knifed
Through the thick
Shroud-like ends
Of cumulous & thunderhead.

Long ago, I made
God's grace out of that light—
A sign, written on heaven,
Of heaven's love for earth.

When I was young,
The world was
Nothing like the world.

That's innocence.
Many of us live in it still.
It's general.

Yet how to reconcile
Such a conceit in any
of Negation's terrible cities?

I am weary of God's love.
I want human love,

Far from the magnificent
Insular cloud-lights
That blaze from stratospheres.

I long for the earthly, guilty
Radiance in your eyes. Little one.

www.ingramcontent.com/pod-product-compliance
Lightning Source LLC
Chambersburg PA
CBHW060406030726
47497CB00003B/869